A

ABT: About

AFAIK: As far as I know

AFK: Away from keyboard

B

B4: Before

BC: Because

BFD: Big freaking deal

BOGO: Buy one get one

BRB: Be right back

BRT: Be right there

BTS: Behind the scenes

BTW: By the way

BYOB: Bring your own beer

D

DAE: Does anyone else?

F

FOMO: Fear of missing out

FTFY: Fixed that for you

FTW: For the win

FUBAR: F***** up beyond all recognition

FWIF: For what it's worth

FWIW: For what it's worth

G

GG: Good game

GTG/G2G: Got to go

H

H8: Hate

HBD: Happy birthday

HMU: Hit me up

I

ICYMI: In case you missed it

IDC: I don't care

IDGAF: I don't give a f***

IDK: I don't know

IKR: I know right

IMHO: In my humble opinion

IMO: In my opinion

IRL: In real life

ISO: In search of

IYKWIM: If you know what I mean

IYKYK: If you know you know

J

JIC: Just in case

JK: Just kidding

JW: Just wondering

L

LMAO: Laughing my a** off

LMK: Let me know

LOL: Laugh out loud

M

MYOB: Mind your own business

N

NBD: No big deal

NGL: Not gonna lie

NVM: Nevermind

P

PLZ: please

POV: Point of view

R

RN: Right now

ROFL: Rolling on the floor laughing

S

SMH: Shaking my head

SNAFU: Situation normal, all f***** up

SRY: sorry

STFU: Shut the f*** up

SUP: what's up?

T

TBA: To be announced

TBD: To be decided

TBF: To be frank

TBH: To be honest

TGIF: Thank goodness it's Friday

TL;DR: Too long, didn't read

TLC: Tender loving care

TMI: Too much information

2NITE: tonight

TTYL: Talk to you later

TW: Trigger warning

W

W/E: Whatever

WTF: What the f***

WYD: What are you doing?

WYSIWYG: What you see is what you get

Business text abbreviations

    1. AKA: Also known as

2. ASAP: As soon as possible

3. COB: Close of business

4. DIY: Do it yourself

5. EOD: End of day

6. FAQ: Frequently asked question

7. FYI: For your information

8. LMGTFY: Let me Google that for you

9. N/A: Not applicable or not available

10. NP: No problem

11. NSFW: Not safe for work

12. OMW: On my way

13. OOO: Out of office

14. TIA: Thanks in advance

15. WDYT: What do you think?

16. WFH: Work from home

17. WYGAM: When you get a minute

Social media text abbreviations

1. AMA: Ask me anything

2. DM: Direct message

3. ELI5: Explain like I'm 5

4. FB: Facebook

5. FBF: Flashback Friday

6. FF: Follow Friday

7. HMU: Hit me up

8. IG: Instagram

9. IM: Instant message

10. LI: LinkedIn

11. MFW: My feeling when

12. OOTD: Outfit of the day

13. OP: Original post

14. PM: Private message

15. QOTD: Quote of the day

16. RT: Retweet

17. SMP: Social media platform

18. TBT: Throwback Thursday

19. TIL: Today I learned

20. YT: YouTube

Romantic text abbreviations

1. ILY: I love you

2. MCM: Man crush Monday

3. WCW: Woman crush Wednesday

4. BF: Boyfriend

5. GF: Girlfriend

6. BAE: Before anyone else

7. LYSM: Love you so much

8. PDA: Public display of affection

9. LTR: Longterm relationship

10. DTR: Define the relationship

11. LDR: Long-distance relationship

12. XOXO: Hugs and kisses

13. OTP: One true pairing

14. LOML: Love of m+y life

Text abbreviations, text slang, internet acronyms, SMS language, emoji, and emoticons! Digital conversing is extremely common in today's world, as a human species we are always looking for ways to simplify things in order to save some extra time and make it easier for everyone to understand. This is seen largely in digital conversing. Minimizing the number of letters required to make a word or creating a completely different word that is significantly smaller than the original keeping the same meaning, as well as, using icons to express something without actually having to type it out.

We've all done or at least experienced this while digitally talking to someone, however, if you find that you're not fully educated in what seems to be the new way of communicating, don't worry because you're definitely not alone.

How To Use Text Abbreviations

Sometimes, text abbreviations just make sense. They're especially helpful when you're trying to keep your texts within a certain character limit, or when you're using very common abbreviations that don't need to be written out. Using a text message abbreviation in the right way can also help you break through to consumers and speak to them in a natural way, especially if you're reaching out for eCommerce markting initiatives

Here are examples of where text abbreviations fit naturally within the body of the message.

Example 1:

Thank you! Your customer service request has been logged. A specialist will reach out by EOD.

Example 2:

ICYMI: Storewide sale this weekend only. Show this text at the counter for an additional 10% off. BTW, store hours are 9AM-7PM Sat and Sun.

Example 3:

TGIF! Celebrate the start of the weekend at [RESTAURANT NAME]. Show this text for two-for-one appetizers.

Example 4:

NOTICE: We've had to delay our event today due to weather. A new day is TBD, and we'll let you know as soon as it's decided!

Example 5:

HBD! Celebrate your big day with 25% off your next order with code [NAME][DATE].

Best Practices for Sending Mass Texts with Abbreviations

These are merely a few examples of how you can use a text abbreviation to establish a rapport with your customers when sending **automated text messages**. No matter how you decide to use text shorthand, try to keep these guidelines in mind.

1. Keep it simple

Because text slang and text message abbreviations can be personal, you don't want to get caught trying to use abbreviations that don't quite make sense — especially when you're sending business text messages. Sticking with the classics, like using BTW to say by the way, is always a good idea. Also, don't try to cram too many letters into one abbreviation. If it gets too cluttered, it loses the purpose of simplifying what you're trying to say.

2. Stay professional

Definitely avoid abbreviations with foul language in them when you're sending business text messages. It's already hard to convey tone through text, and adding edgy abbreviations just complicates this task. Play it safe and stick to family-friendly slang.

Add media to your texts

The great thing about text message marketing is you're not limited to only text! By sending an MMS message you can actually attach an image or a GIF. If you're sending a TGIF appetizer special, for example, attaching an image to the mobile coupon can help you look more professional and compelling.

Avoid Abbreviation Mistakes

Even though text abbreviations can be useful, it's also quite easy to go wrong when trying to use them. Part of the reason for this is that slang changes rapidly, and using a text message abbreviation that's no longer in vogue can make you stand out—in the wrong way. Avoid these mistakes in order to come across in your best light when texting.

1. Watch out for dated slang

What's in style and what's dated is obviously subjective, so part of this really relies on your knowing your audience. Just as an example: it would probably come across as out-of-touch to millennials if you incorporate numbers into your abbreviations. Common abbreviations like "Good 2 c u" or "Come 2 our bar 2nite 4 a gr8 time" probably aren't going to convince many younger people that you know what you're talking about.

It's a good idea to run your abbreviations by a few different people on your marketing team before using them. Try to get the best sense for your audience, and scrap any abbreviations you're unsure about.

2. Don't overuse abbreviations

You don't want a whole text full of abbreviations, because that's just going to make people feel like they're deciphering a code. As a guideline, it's safest to stick with one well-placed abbreviation in your entire text message. If you're trying to abbreviate because you're running out of room, consider sending a shortened link to a website that can more fully explain the details you're trying to get across. Or, send an MMS with a photo that contains more information.

Text Abbreviations As a Marketing Asset

Using a text abbreviation in the right way gives your company the chance to speak casually with your customers and show them you truly understand their language. Just make sure your abbreviations are simple and common enough that people actually understand what you're saying. If you're ever in doubt, opt for a full-length version of the word you're trying to shorten.

Emoji	Name	Meaning
😂	Face with Tears of Joy	Extreme happiness or laughter
❤️	Red Heart	Love (red by default, but meaning is same for any color)
🤣	Rolling on the Floor Laughing	Intense or hysterical laughter
👍	Thumbs Up Sign	Well done, good job, or approval
😭	Loudly Crying Face	Uncontrollable tears, perhaps due to sadness or joy
🙏	Person with Folded Hands	Prayer, thank you, and sometimes a high five
😘	Face Throwing a Kiss	Kissing someone, or general expression of love
🥰	Smiling Face with Hearts	Love or affection
😍	Smiling Face with Heart-Eyes	Love or adoration
😊	Smiling Face with Smiling Eyes	Positive or happy
🎉	Party Popper	Celebration or congratulations
😁	Grinning Face with Smiling Eyes	Glowing, beaming happiness
💕	Two Hearts	Love is in the air
🥺	Pleading Face	Adoration, bashful, or pleading

😅	Smiling Face with Open Mouth and Cold Sweat	Relief, nerves, or excitement
🔥	Fire	Hot or excellent
😊	Smiling Face	Happy or positive
🤦	Face Palm	Frustrated or dumbfounded
❤️	Heart Suit	Love
🤷	Shrug	Indifference or unknowing
🙄	Face With Rolling Eyes	Sarcasm or boredom
😆	Smiling Face with Open Mouth and Tightly-Closed Eyes	Great excitement or happiness
🤗	Hugging Face	Hugging (love and support) or jazz hands (enthusiasm)
😉	Winking Face	Joking or being cheeky
🎂	Birthday Cake	Celebration
🤔	Thinking Face	Pondering or questioning
👏	Clapping Hands Sign	Round of applause in celebration
🙂	Slightly Smiling Face	Happy, but often used ironically
😳	Flushed Face	Embarrassed, surprised, or flattered
🥳	Partying Face	Celebration or joy
😎	Smiling Face with Sunglasses	Cool or confident
👌	OK Hand Sign	Okay or correct
💜	Purple Heart	Love
😔	Pensive Face	Reflective or remorseful

	Flexed Biceps	Strength or fitness
	Sparkles	Positive, happy, or celebration
	Sparkling Heart	Extra special love, sometimes playful
	Eyes	Shifty or sneaky, sometimes flirtatious
	Face Savoring Delicious Food	Cheeky, poking fun, or enjoying food
	Smirking Face	Mischievous or flirting
	Crying Face	Upset or in pain
	Backhand Index Pointing Right	Pointing to the right
	Growing Heart	Love or increasing affection
	Weary Face	Distressed, drained, or deep enjoyment
	Hundred Points Symbol	100 percent approval
	Rose	Romance or to be used on a special occasion
	Revolving Hearts	A whirlwind of love
	Balloon	Celebration or congratulations
	Blue Heart	Love
	Smiling Face with Open Mouth	Happiness
	Pouting Face	Annoyed or angry
	Bouquet	Appreciation or happiness
	Face with Stuck-Out Tongue and Winking Eye	Fun, joking, or cheeky
	See-No-Evil Monkey	Hiding, cringing, or in disbelief

	Crossed Fingers	Wishing luck
	Smiling Face with Open Mouth and Smiling Eyes	Great happiness
	Drooling Face	Desiring something or delirious
	Person Raising Both Hands in Celebration	Celebrating with hands in the air
	Zany Face	Silly, fun, or goofy
	Heavy Heart Exclamation Mark Ornament	Emphasized love
	Grinning Face	Elevated happiness
	Kiss Mark	A seductive kiss
	Skull	Death or an extreme reaction to something
	Backhand Index Pointing Down	Pointing down
	Broken Heart	Grief, loss, or longing
	Relieved Face	Content or calm
	Beating Heart	Love
	Grinning Face with Star Eyes	Amazed, impressed, or excited
	Upside Down Face	Silliness, often used for irony or sarcasm
	Grimacing Face	Tense, nervous, or awkward
	Face Screaming in Fear	Shocked or scared
	Sleeping Face	Tired or bored
	Face with Hand Over Mouth	Laughter or cheekiness
	Neutral Face	Neutral, irritated, or unamused
	Sun with Face	Radiant, happy, or

☺	Neutral Face	Neutral, irritated, or unamused
☺	Sun with Face	Radiant, happy, or positive
☺	Unamused Face	Annoyed, skeptic, or irritated
☺	Smiling Face with Halo	Angelic or innocent
❀	Cherry Blossom	Love or to be used on a special occasion
👿	Smiling Face With Horns	Cheeky, naughty, or mischief
🎵	Multiple Musical Notes	Three eighth notes, for singing or music
✌	Victory Hand	Peace or success
🎊	Confetti Ball	Celebration or congratulations
☺	Hot Face	Overheating or flirty
☹	Disappointed Face	Disappointed, upset, or remorse
💚	Green Heart	Love
☀	Sun	Sunny, warm, or hot
🖤	Black Heart	Love or sorrow
💰	Money Bag	Money or wealth
😘	Kissing Face With Closed Eyes	Puckering for a kiss
👑	Crown	Royalty, success, or praise
🎁	Wrapped Gift	Celebration or surprise
💥	Collision	Explosion, surprise, or excitement
🙋	Happy Person Raising One Hand	Waving or asking a question
☹	Frowning Face	Sad, concerned, or disappointed
😑	Expressionless Face	Bored, indifferent, or pausing to collect thoughts
😵	Woozy Face	Drunk, dazed, or confused
👈	Backhand Index Pointing Left	Pointing to the left

😒	Unamused Face	Annoyed, skeptic, or irritated
😇	Smiling Face with Halo	Angelic or innocent
🌸	Cherry Blossom	Love or to be used on a special occasion
😈	Smiling Face With Horns	Cheeky, naughty, or mischief
🎶	Multiple Musical Notes	Three eighth notes, for singing or music
✌	Victory Hand	Peace or success
🎊	Confetti Ball	Celebration or congratulations
🥵	Hot Face	Overheating or flirty
😞	Disappointed Face	Disappointed, upset, or remorse
💚	Green Heart	Love
☀	Sun	Sunny, warm, or hot
🖤	Black Heart	Love or sorrow
💰	Money Bag	Money or wealth
😚	Kissing Face With Closed Eyes	Puckering for a kiss
👑	Crown	Royalty, success, or praise
🎁	Wrapped Gift	Celebration or surprise
💥	Collision	Explosion, surprise, or excitement
🙋	Happy Person Raising One Hand	Waving or asking a question
☹	Frowning Face	Sad, concerned, or disappointed
😑	Expressionless Face	Bored, indifferent, or pausing to collect thoughts
🥴	Woozy Face	Drunk, dazed, or confused
👈	Backhand Index Pointing Left	Pointing to the left
💩	Pile of Poo	Poo, bad, or silliness
✅	Check Mark Button	Approval or verification

Printed in Great Britain
by Amazon